GW00706175

WITH LOVE TO

·····································

FROM

·····································

A Lifetime of Promises Series
FAITH
©Scandinavia Publishing House
Drejervej 15.3 DK-Copenhagen NV
Denmark

www.scanpublishing.dk
info@scanpublishing.dk

Selection of Scripture
by Carol A. Kauffman
Design by Ben Alex

ISBN 978-87-7132-012-1

A Lifetime of Promises

Faith

Quotes from the Holy Bible

scandinavia

The Scriptures say
That no one who has faith
Will be disappointed.

Romans 10:11 CEV

In You
Our fathers trusted;
They trusted and
You delivered them.

PSALM 22:4 NASB

Be strong and
Let your heart take courage,
All you who hope
In the LORD.

Psalm 31:24 NASB

Teach me
Your way, O LORD;
I will walk in Your truth;
Unite my heart
To fear Your name.

Psalm 86:11 NASB

How blessed
Is the man
Who has
Made the LORD
His trust.

Psalm 40:4a NASB

Abraham
Never waivered
In believing God's promise,
His faith grew stronger,
And in this he brought
Glory to God.

Romans 4:20 NLT

He was fully convinced
That God is able to do
Whatever he promises.

ROMANS 4:21 NLT

I am sure that
Nothing can separate us
From God's love –
Not life or death,
Not angels or spirits,
Not the present or the future.

ROMANS 8:38 CEV

Set your mind
On the things above,
Not on the things
That are on earth.

COLOSSIANS 3:2 NASB

Nothing
In all creation
Can separate us
From God's love for us
In Christ Jesus.

ROMANS 8:39 CEV

I pray that God,
Who gives hope,
Will bless you with
Complete happiness and peace
Because of your faith.

ROMANS 15:13A CEV

May the power
Of the Holy Spirit
Fill you with hope.

ROMANS 15:13B CEV

And I now live
By faith in the Son of God,
Who loved me
And gave his life for me.

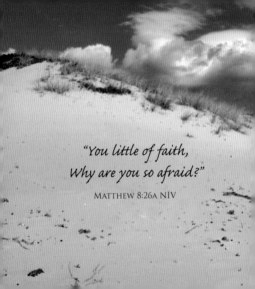

"You little of faith,
Why are you so afraid?"

MATTHEW 8:26A NIV

Fix you thoughts
On what is true,
And honourable,
And right, and pure,
And lovely, and
Admirable.

P‌HILIPPIANS 4:8B NLT

I know the one
In whom I trust,
And I am sure
That he is able to guard
What I have entrusted to him
Until the day of his return.

2 TIMOTHY 1:12B NLT

"Look, I am
Placing in Zion
A choice and
Precious cornerstone.
No one who has faith
In that one
Will be disappointed."

1 PETER 2:6b CEV

"If you remain faithful
Even when facing death,
I will give you
The crown of life."

Revelation 2:10b NLT

By faith
We have been made
Acceptable to God.
And now, because of
Our Lord Jesus Christ,
We live at peace
With God.

ROMANS 5:1 CEV

Without faith

No one can

Please God.

Hebrews 11:6a CEV

Let us hold tightly
Without wavering
To the hope we affirm,
For God can be trusted
To keep his promise.

Hebrews 10:23 NLT

We must believe
That God is real
And that he rewards everyone
Who searches for him.

Hebrews 11:6b CEV

Anything
Is possible
If a person
Believes.

MARK 9:23b NLT

Faith is the confidence
That what we hope for
Will actually happen.

Hebrews 11:1a NLT

It gives us

Assurance

About what

We cannot see.

HEBREWS 11:1b NLT

Nothing
Is as wonderful
As knowing
Christ Jesus
My Lord.

PHILIPPIANS 3:8a CEV

Now all glory to God,
Who is able,
Through his mighty power
At work within us,
To accomplish infinitely more
Than we might
Ask or think.

EPHESIANS 3:20 NLT

And the peace of God,
Which surpasses
All comprehension,
Will guard your
Hearts and minds
In Christ Jesus.

Philippians 4:7 NASB

"I will bless
Those who
Trust me."

JEREMIAH 17:7 CEV

And my God will supply
All your needs
According to His riches
In glory in Christ Jesus.

PHILIPPIANS 4:19 NASB

Walk in a manner
Worthy of the Lord,
To please Him
In all respects.

Colossians 1:10a NASB

For you have died
And your life is hidden
With Christ in God.

COLOSSIANS 3:3 NASB

Oh, how great

Are God's riches

And wisdom

And knowledge!

ROMANS 11:33A NLT

Three things
Will last forever –
Faith, hope, and love –
And the greatest
Of these is love.

1 Corinthians 13:13 NLT

For the more we suffer
For Christ,
The more God will
Shower us with his comfort
Through Christ.

2 CORINTHIANS 1:5 NLT

Thanks
Be to God
For His
Indescribable
Gift!

2 Corinthians 9:15 NASB

"*Truly, truly,*
I say to you,
He who believes in Me,
The works that I do,
He will do also."

JOHN 14:12A NASB

The Lord isn't slow
Concerning his promises
Like some people
Think he is.

2 PETER 3:9A CEV

In fact, God is patient
Because he wants
Everyone to turn from sin
And no one to be lost.

2 PETER 3:9B CEV

We are certain
That God will hear
Our prayers
When we ask for
What pleases him.

1 JOHN 5:14 CEV

Whoever has
The Son has life;
Whoever does not
Have God's Son
Does not have life.

1 JOHN 5:12 NLT

He has told you, O man,
What is good;
And what does the LORD
Require of you
But to do justice,
To love kindness,
And to walk humbly
With your God?

MICAH 6:8 NASB

But speaking
The truth in love,
We are to grow up
In all aspects
Into him who
Is the head,
Even Christ.

EPHESIANS 4:15 NASB

God loved us so much
That he made us alive
With Christ,
And God's wonderful kindness
Is what saves us.

Ephesians 2:4b-5 CEV

God's Spirit
Makes us loving,
Happy, peaceful, patient,
Kind, good, faithful.

GALATIANS 5:22 CEV

For whatever
Is born of God
Overcomes the world;
And this is the victory
That has overcome the world –
Our faith.

1 John 5:4 NASB

He who believes in me,
The works that I do,
He will do also;
And greater works
Than these he will do;
Because I go to the Father.

John 14:12b NASB

If you trust the Lord,
You will never miss out
On any good thing.

PSALM 34:10B CEV

But if we live
In the light,
As God does,
We share in life
With each other.

1 JOHN 1:7A CEV

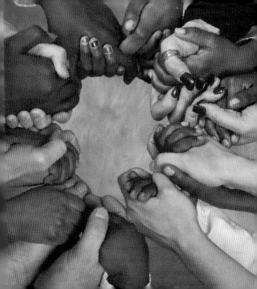

Trust in the Lord
With all your heart
And lean not
On your own
Understanding.

PROVERBS 3:5A NIV

Trust in
The Lord always,
For the Lord God
Is the eternal Rock.

Isaiah 26:4 NLT